Where Is Radar?
by Elayne Palmer

WINN PUBLICATIONS, FL

Hi! My name is Elayne, and I have a cat named Radar. When I first got Radar, he liked to sleep a lot! And he slept everywhere!

As he started to grow up, he liked to try to play "hide and seek." (He thought I couldn't see him!)

Then one day, I walked into my house and I couldn't find Radar any where! Could you help me find him?

Where's Radar?

There he is!!!

I can't find him again! Can you help me find Radar?

There he is. You found him!

Now where did Radar go?

There he is! He can't trick you!!

Can you find Radar again?
I can't see him.

You are so good at finding Radar!

Oh, no! He's hiding again. Where's Radar?

There he is!

I give up! I can't find Radar. Can you?

He's in the middle of the pillows. Silly Radar!

Radar is playing hide and seek again. Where's Radar hiding?

There he is!
Radar, you are a
smart cat!

It's time for Radar to eat. Where is that cat?

You found him!
You are such a smart helper!!

Radar! Radar!
I really can't find him.
Can you?

There he is! Thank you! You can always find Radar.

Radar, this is the last time! Where are you?

There he is. You're the best cat-finder in the world!

Radar, I'm so glad you're in my bed! I am going to take a nap and rest. I'm tired of playing hide and seek.

2023 COPYRIGHT ELAYNE PALMER

ILLUSTRATION BY:
AUBREY PALMER

PHOTOS BY:
ELAYNE PALMER
CAROL PAPKA

ALL RIGHTS RESERVED.
NO PART OF THIS BOOK MAY BE
REPRODUCED, STORED IN A RETRIEVAL SYSTEM OR TRANSMITTED BY ANY MEANS WITHOUT THE WRITTEN PERMISSION OF THE PUBLISHER.

ISBN: 979-8-9858001-1-1

PUBLISHED BY:
WINN PUBLICATIONS
WINNPUBLICATIONS.COM
FLORIDA, USA

Milton Keynes UK
Ingram Content Group UK Ltd.
UKRC030233041123
431843UK00012B/48